MICHAEL WILKEY

HOW TO STOP SMOKING FOR GOOD

Matador
9 De Montfort Mews
Leicester LE1 7FW, UK
Tel: (+44) 116 255 9311 / 9312
Email: books@troubador.co.uk
Web: www.troubador.co.uk/matador

ISBN 1 904744 74 5

Permission to reproduce "Nicotine" extracted from
From Comets to Cocaine by Dr Rudolph Steiner has kindly been
given by Rudolf Steiner Press, London
Published 2000 (ISBN 1-85584 88-X)

Web: www.michaelwilkey.com

Cover design by Tetes a Tetes

Typeset in 10pt Stempel Garamond by Troubador Publishing Ltd, Leicester, UK
Printed by The Cromwell Press, Trowbridge, Wilts, UK

Matador is an imprint of Troubador Publishing

Thanks to the people who have encouraged and assisted me with the production of this book, especially David, Janet, Trevor, Jessica, Philip, Richard, Helene, Daniel and Peter.

CONTENTS

INTRODUCTION

Smoking is a delicate and sensitive subject. You are holding a little book that will show you how to help yourself stop smoking pleasantly and permanently. It has been designed for people who have reached the point where they *want* to stop, so if you are not yet at this stage, put the book away for another day. You are not being told to stop – that must be your decision – but you will be shown a simple, encouraging and straightforward method of how to go about it. Only you can stop yourself smoking.

The author is a non-smoker who used to smoke and has experience helping and encouraging others to stop for good with a simple step-by-step plan. You will be helped to formulate your own strong motivation to stop smoking, and then discover incentives that will encourage you towards a healthier and happier nicotine-free life.

"Don't tell me to stop smoking, tell me *how* to stop smoking" is the understandable request of many smokers, but it is not easy to find anyone to tell you how. Well-intentioned doctors will prescribe patches, sedatives, pills and potions, nasal sprays and give words of encouragement, but are rarely able to offer anything in the way of practical advice as to *how* we can help ourselves. This is very strange – large amounts of money have been spent on encouraging people to stop smoking, on warning them of the dangers, on cancer research, on finding substitutes, but considering the enormity of the problem there is a severe lack of practical advice on *how* to stop. This book does tell you how, and it gives useful exercises that are of great benefit both in deciding to stop and ensuring that you never start again.

To stop smoking is one of life's big decisions; you have been brave enough to pick up and start reading this books... stick with it and you *will* become a non-smoker.

PART ONE

Smoking is a habit that just does not make sense. This book will help you stop of your own volition, in your own time, with no nasty side effects and no regrets. You will feel 100% confident that you will never want to put a cigarette in your mouth again and your biggest wonder will be that you didn't stop earlier.

The moment arrives when you have had enough of smoking and decide you want to stop, many people are fortunate and are able to do this without any problems, and others require some help and seek advice. A whole industry has arisen which offers advice in the form of books, videos, patches, herbal tobaccos, gums, hypnotherapy, or psychotherapy but very few people will actually tell you HOW to stop.

Here you will find a simple and natural method that can be followed by anyone, anywhere. No patches or herbal tobaccos, etc are used so that you know you are stopping as a result of your own efforts and are not simply shifting your dependence from one place to another. Because you have stopped from your own volition you will be better resolved not to start again and with this method you will save yourself a fortune.

There is a step by step plan which unfolds as you read

through the book and it is up to you to choose the right moment to quit. This book does not offer a miracle cure but will help you to help yourself. It is recommended that you take your time and read slowly, your active involvement is required and it is necessary that you do each of the exercises. Some of these require writing so you will need to have a note book handy. The simple and gentle exercises given as part of the plan are designed to strengthen both your resolve to quit and your ability to break the habit, they will take a minimum of five minutes each day. The more you put in the more you will take out.

The chances are that the idea of stopping is a little bit frightening; you wonder whether you can stop and whether life will be worth living once you have. It is also possible that you are in the position where you both desire to quit and not quit at the same time. Don't worry, all that's asked at this stage is that YOU WANT TO STOP, so sit back and take it easy.

There is not much point in reading this book unless you want to stop, this should be made very clear as there is then no need for the writer to help you make what must be your own decision. You are not being told "what" to do but being shown "how" to carry out your resolve, and there is a big difference. If you know that you want to remove cigarettes from your life for ever then you have already taken a big step in the right direction, this step needs to be followed by another — so read on. When you know what you want you have a good chance of getting it.

It is important for you to become as clear as possible in your own mind exactly why you wish to stop. In the next few pages suggestions are given to help stimulate your thoughts; it will be good if in addition you can collect some personal reasons that are not included here.

Hopefully you will have a relaxed state of mind and body while reading so feel free to smoke.* Yes, really, feel free to smoke, it's a very friendly method! Better still you are free to stop at any stage.

Please remember this book is totally on your side, you want to stop smoking and the book will gently help and encourage. It is not trying to be the most sensational book on the market and deliberately avoids making claims, reading it is certainly not a weakness and accepting a little help and advice is actually a sign of strength. Many smokers are reluctant to even pick up books of this nature, yet alone open them. Getting this far really does mean that you are well on the road to improving the quality of your life.

REASONS FOR STOPPING

It is not difficult to come up with a long list of excellent reasons for stopping smoking and we will spend some time finding as many of them as possible.

The following few pages will stimulate your thoughts so that you can discover your own unique list of reasons. This is essential to building your motivation and enforcing your resolve. Time is well spent discovering exactly "Why you

---

*If you have already quit don't start again.

3

want to stop" and this will provide a solid foundation upon which you can build.

Ask yourself:

"Why do I want to stop?"

"What is my main reason for stopping?"

"What are my other reasons?"

Spend time on this and formulate these reasons as clearly as possible. We can not make progress by living with our heads buried in the sand and avoiding the problem but only by looking directly at everything involved with smoking. (In our case we are hiding with our heads in clouds of smoke and thus putting the problem out of sight.)

To stop smoking is not an entirely painless process; you have to go through the eye of the needle to come out stronger on the other side. You will read several times here that "only you can stop yourself smoking", it's the obvious truth and you will have to face it. The largest obstacle to stopping is a reluctance to see clearly what we are doing and reading the next few pages will help remove this obstacle. The greatest incentive to becoming a non smoker is the knowledge that it will improve the quality of your life.

FINANCIAL

The growing cost of smoking is a perfectly good and obvious reason for stopping and it applies to all but the extremely rich.

Part One: Reasons to Stop Smoking

On a piece of paper work out just how much you are spending on cigarettes.

How much is this costing you per week, per month, per year?

How much is this costing over your lifetime?

What percentage of your total expenditure goes on tobacco?

Are you spending more on tobacco than food? (Some people do)

How will the quality of life improve for you and your family once you have stopped?

You are probably paying income tax on your earnings of some 25% or more, add this to the total and you will be able to find out how many days/weeks a year you are working to pay for smoking.

In addition to buying cigarettes you are paying your dentist to clean tar stains of your teeth and your health and insurance premiums are almost certainly higher because you are a smoker. Smokers take more time off work due to sickness.

There is really little more to say about the monetary cost of smoking! Over your life time it might well be costing the price of your car and possibly your house. The fiscal reasons are absolutely clear and not smoking will represent paying fewer taxes. Next time you look at a politician on the television wearing yet another new suit try to work out who paid for it.

When you purchase cigarettes you are not receiving anything worth having, you are far better of without them and once you stop you will certainly have more spare money. This is a good, sensible and powerful reason for stopping. Not many people go out and buy a whole years supply of tobacco all in one go, perhaps because they are frightened to face up to just how much money they are spending and perhaps because they think they are going to stop very shortly.

Here is a list of some of the people involved in a vast industry who encourage you to continue smoking because they want your money. They are definitely not on your side and do everything they can to see that you continue with the habit for the rest of your life. They have a vested interest and prosper from your habit:

- Tobacco farmers (amazingly some tobacco farmers in Europe are still receiving subsidies from the EEC)
- Cigarette manufacturers and their shareholders
- Advertising companies
- Tobacconists and vending machine manufacturers
- Shippers, distributors and salespeople

Here is a list of some people who also make money because you smoke but will strongly advise you to stop.

- Governments
- Nurses/Dentists/Doctors/Surgeons
- Cancer research agencies.

Tobacco really is the silliest of drugs; you part with money and get absolutely nothing worthwhile in return and you can bet that the price will keep on going up and up.

There is also a huge industry centred on people who want to stop smoking which includes books like this, gums, patches, medicines, therapies, videos, health farms etc.

Politicians enjoying their five course meals, limousines and fancy suits owe you and your fellow smokers a big thank you. You can be sure that they will soon be pushing the price up even higher.

The financial costs of smoking provide an excellent reason for you to stop because you will save a fortune.

HEALTH REASONS

It is generally agreed that the biggest improvement you can make to your health is to stop smoking; this is followed by ensuring that you have plenty of exercise in fresh air, have a healthy diet and avoid stress.

Over the years you will certainly have gathered enormous amounts of information on the harmful and damaging effects of smoking without needing to hear more of the same here. The information you have will include endless horrific details of lung cancer, blindness, respiratory diseases, tooth and gum decay, etc, etc. If you need even more convincing of the harm tobacco does there are plenty of books and internet information is easily available. The grim fact is that tobacco kills more Americans (a country where smoking has decreased) each year than alcohol, cocaine, crack, heroin, homicide, suicide, car accidents and aids COMBINED!!! Every packet of cigarettes now carries a health warning and gruesome pictures but these scare tactics have not worked well, smokers develop a knack of blocking out the information they do not wish to receive and young people continue to start smoking.

These frightening reasons are very powerful, but they are simply not powerful enough, otherwise you would have become disgusted and stopped by now. It is quite possible for smokers to consider themselves somehow "Super Human" and live believing that the dangers of smoking only apply to other people.

Our approach will be to focus on the health benefits that come from quitting; these are major and immediate at all ages and provide excellent reasons for becoming a non-smoker as soon as possible. The best motivation to stop smoking will come from all the positive reasons that you can discover. The moment that you quit your health will improve and the beneficial effects of not smoking will be with you for the rest of your longer active life.

Here is the good news:

- The risk of having a heart attack is decreased by 50% within 24 hours of quitting smoking.

- Smokers cough disappears within three months of quitting for most people.

- After only two years of abstinence from tobacco the risk of heart disease is decreased to about the level of non smokers.

- Smell and taste senses improve within days and

so does your self-esteem.

- Risk of lung cancer is decreased by 80—90% after 15 years of abstinence.

- Even stopping at 60 years of age is said by the British Medical Association to give an extra three years of active life.

The simple message is that your health will improve radically as soon as you stop smoking. This is the good news and provides a wonderful incentive to be a non-smoker.

Without toxins in your blood, cuts and bruises heal more quickly and menstrual pains are reduced.

You will be better able to undertake sports such as mountain climbing at higher altitudes and diving at depths that are difficult for smokers.

Find time to do your own research and gather as many positive reasons as you can, it's your life, your health and your responsibility. It's the positive reasons that will convince you stopping is the right decision, you will find tons of interesting up to date information in libraries and on the internet, it can become an absorbing subject.

THE CON

We are never deceived; we deceive ourselves
(J. W. Goethe)

The first two reasons provide plenty of motivation for stopping but for many the Con aspect is even greater, it is also more difficult for many people to accept. Nobody likes to discover that they have been the victim of a confidence trick but this is what has happened to millions of intelligent well educated people.

Advertising works. That's why tobacco companies spend so much money on it and you see large amounts in cinemas, on posters, in magazines and rather oddly at sports events. It is extraordinary to think that someone can convince others that cigarette smoke in their lungs can somehow make them run faster, play football better or drive a car faster.

The sophisticated marketing techniques are not just getting you to look at pictures of their products but to actively think about them, to interact and to get involved. People pressure in the western world has brought about a decrease in the amount of money that can be spent on advertising so the companies have turned their attention and resources to developing countries. The old forms of advertising have been replaced by brand sharing, product placement in films, subliminal adverts, the use of theme music, the association of their brand with a colour and surrogate products sponsoring sports events and personalities. The amount of smoking shown in movies has increased since cigarette advertisements have been banned from billboards and an "R" certificate is now being proposed to indicate a film that shows people smoking.

When we look at the enormous size of the tobacco industry and how much money is involved we can see why some of the world's cleverest people have been employed by these companies to get people hooked and keep them hooked, not only to cigarettes in general but to particular brands. The teams employed include doctors, scientists, psychologists, psychiatrists and artists who are aware that the physical addiction to tobacco is less important than psychological dependence. They employ every dirty trick they can think up to keep people hooked. Lawyers work in tandem with doctors to argue that nicotine and the tars in tobacco are not harmful; their vested interest is to take your money and at the same time destroy your health.

The chances are that you never meet any of these people who somehow manage to live with themselves and their families and lead apparently normal lives while knowing they are responsible for the death and injury of thousands upon thousands of people. You can be sure that they know enough about the dangerous affects of cigarettes that when they come home from a day of promoting their expensive harmful product that they will take care to discourage their own children from ever sampling them.

Millions of highly paid man hours have been devoted to researching and developing a poisonous and addictive product. Millions more man hours are used to make this unhealthy, ugly product appear attractive. This would seem to be an impossible task but it has been all too cleverly accomplished by companies with virtually unlimited resources and low morality. These people are not to be underestimated; the tobacco companies are licensed to maim and kill. They have absolutely no interest in helping you to quit and try to make their products, which contain tar, nicotine and carbon monoxide, as addictive as possible. The big companies agree that "cigarettes can be characterised as addictive and hard for some people to stop" and that "cigarettes should not be regarded as safe" but their highly paid executives still maintain that their products do not cause lung cancer.

Tobacco manufacturers employ devilishly clever methods to snare people, particularly children and teenagers, into smoking with tricks such as handing out free cigarettes. These companies know that young people are easily addicted and that just four free cigarettes can be enough to hook someone for life. They also give free entrance to discotheques on production of empty cigarette packets and do everything they can to convince vulnerable young girls and boys that smoking is both respectable and glamorous through advertising and sponsoring sports and music events.

A handful of enormous multi-national companies have now cornered the entire world tobacco industry and are loyal to no one except their shareholders. They work closely with political parties and are in league with national governments. They have made themselves so powerful that it is a waste of time and energy to fight them; all that can be done is to ignore their dreadful products and to keep them away from the young. Their products kill and injure far more people than wars and land mines making them the world's biggest killers. Of course they do not see it that way at all, like all con men they fall for there own tricks and lies and amazingly manage to go to work each day convinced that they are doing something worthwhile for the world.

Tobacco is legal and it is the job of these companies to make their dangerous product attractive, glamorous and wonderful. Illegal drugs like heroine, crack and cocaine are marketed in exactly the same way with discounts offered and free samples given to people to encourage them to start. We are looking for positive reasons to stop smoking but it would be wrong to ignore the dreadful forces operating in the tobacco industry. If some people are capable of designing and colouring land mines so that children are tempted to pick them up as toys to play with then it is possible that something just as ghastly is happening with cigarette packets.

Sorry, but if you smoke it's because you have been conned, sold a dud, tricked, suckered. The wonderful thing is that we are able to walk away from these people, never to give them another cent. First you have to see that without you realizing it they have managed to enslave you, and then you can experience the joy of walking away from them never to return. It really is amazingly clever that they can tempt people into such an unhealthy, expensive and unpleasant habit. They have used tricks and lies. This book will look for the honest truth of what is happening, the big cigarette companies are Goliath and we are David's. David won by using courage and the right strategy.

One of the cigarette company's tricks is to try to convince people that it is very difficult to stop smoking. It is not, it's surprisingly easy and pleasant when you are honest with yourself and employ an optimistic and positive attitude. You are not being asked to do the impossible, millions of people just like you have successfully stopped for good. Starting to smoke and continuing to smoke is hard because nobody likes their first cigarette, they taste horrible.

We have started to look at what is happening to us and so we are on the road to doing something about it. It's not a case of fighting or blaming these cigarette companies as that just takes our energy and gives it to them. The trick is to stop, create something new and our family and friends will then also stop and the companies will have no more slaves. They know their days are numbered and that they are on the way out which is why they are behaving like caged animals. Sadly they are using their nasty tricks on innocent young people in countries that are still in process of development such as India and China. Years ago the British Empire was able to find medical doctors to certify that opium was not addictive and it appears that such people are still around justifying another despicable trade.

Oh no, the tobacco companies don't want you to stop, they live well of smokers. Try taking a copy of this book to your tobacconist and suggest they sell it alongside their nicotine products, take a copy to the international airport and suggest the same thing. (Perhaps they will have a change of heart and start stocking it, that would be wonderful.) They will happily sell you cigarettes by the thousand but they know that they are unhealthy and smelly things and will not allow you to smoke them anywhere near their shop or on the planes for fear of upsetting other passengers.

Everyone in the cigarette business wants you hooked, hooked, hooked, big time, for life. When you realise this you have taken a hard step forward, harder than stopping!

One cigarette makes you want to have another.

SOCIAL STIGMA

Rightly or wrongly smokers are being put into a corner, or even kicked outside, by the majority who don't approve of their habit. They are becoming social outcasts who need to stick together and can be seen during coffee breaks standing in groups, banished from offices and factories stamping their feet to keep warm while they try to light up three cigarettes in ten minutes. New York, Ireland and Norway have now banned smoking from pubs, restaurants and public places, other countries are likely to follow suit and the most famous beaches in Australia are becoming smoke free.

Times are changing; people don't want smokers and the stale lingering smell of cigarettes in their houses or cars and are no longer afraid to say so. Many people don't want smokers near their children as it sets a bad example and smokers can wonder if this is a reason why they are sometimes not sent invitations to social functions

Passive smoking has received a lot of publicity recently and evidence is showing that second hand smoke is very danger-ous. Some people become quite hostile even if they see someone holding a cigarette. Although airports make the purchase of duty free tobacco products simple and attractive finding somewhere to smoke is not, smokers spend time looking for the small badly ventilated smoking room set aside for them where they are treated like second class citi-zens. If these dreadful little smoky rooms were torture chambers the occupants would be entitled to complain. This is a rather miserable way of beginning a daunting long "no smoking" flight and it is bound to induce an increase in stress and nervousness.

It is a discomforting feeling to think that you are the last smoker in your family, office, factory, street, or town. Today smokers are being increasingly judged, excluded and discriminated against in the workplace and sometimes they must forfeit a chance of promotion. Millions of people just like you have improved their lives by stopping; you can too.

Self esteem and confidence increase dramatically when you stop and life is enjoyable without nicotine.

FEEL FREE

One of the biggest reasons to stop brings together elements of fiscal, health, con and social which can be lumped together under the category of "feeling free" from being controlled and becoming mistress/master of your own destiny.

There is a feeling of "victory", of having "won" when you are again a non-smoker and it is uplifting to know that you can operate perfectly well without having to carry a little packet of drugs around with you. Once you have stopped you will feel more alive and have more confidence from knowing that you had the determination and willpower to stop.

For many people the single biggest reason to stop smoking is because they are tired of being controlled and manipulated by tobacco companies, they want to be free of the drug and live with dignity. Addiction means being not free, stopping brings a sense of relief from no longer being manipulated and controlled.

We all admire people who have managed to stop and we believe them when they tell us that life is more pleasant without the props.

MY LIST

You have done some reading and now the time has come for you to pick up your notebook and pen and to start writing down your own list of reasons for wanting to stop. Use the reasons given here to stimulate your own thinking, some of them you may consider trivial or irrelevant, that's fine, but replace them with even better ones of your own.

Start your list with the most important reason working down to the least important and try to differentiate between the positive and the negative. Writing, "When I stop smoking I will live longer" will be more effective than writing, "If I keep on smoking I will die earlier" Both statements are true, just as you can see either a vase or two faces, you have to decide what you want to see.

Writing down your reasons can be an ongoing task as you continue to read through the book and you can include other thoughts, feelings and insights that come to mind. This will stimulate you to think more about the smoking process and to become interested and engaged in what is a most fascinating subject. Have little conversations with people at home and at work, discover why people smoke, why they want to stop, why they have difficulty stopping, and how they have stopped. Go to the internet, the library and gather as much information as you can, the more effort and involvement you can put into this the better. Spend time doing this because it will supply the all important motivation to stop.

＊　　＊　　＊　　＊　　＊

You should now have a note book and a LIST OF EXCEL-LENT REASONS FOR WANTING TO STOP; perhaps you have found so many good ones that choosing one for the top was difficult. They are all good but above all it's the positive reasons that will convince you that it's wise to become a non-smoker.

If you are in the position of having been told by a medical practitioner that you must stop you can still make yourself a list with as many positive reasons as you can find. Stopping is something you can look forward to because it will improve the quality of your life, wasting the rest of your life as a smoker is something to dread.

The list you are making will of course be unique to you and perhaps contain some very personal reasons for wanting to stop, keep it in a safe place as you will need to refer to late on. When you go to someone for help in stopping smoking, whether it is a doctor, councillor, therapist, acupuncturist hypnotist etc, no matter how accomplished they are at the end of the day its YOU that has to muster the motivation and strength to stop. People can give encouragement, offer advice, patches, gums etc. but it is your own positive endeavour that will sustain you, there is no alternative, there is no way round it

By writing down your reasons to stop you have begun to look seriously at what is happening when you smoke and this will help unravel what is really a very mysterious and strange phenomenon. Smokers become used to their ritual of buying, lighting and smoking cigarettes, it is something they take for granted and do repeatedly every day of their lives for years and years without ever sitting down and looking at what is happening.

You can choose to stop because you are disgusted with the habit or because you can see a better life ahead without cigarettes, either way it means change which always involves a certain amount of temporary discomfort. You have the choice of remaining stuck in a love/hate relationship or moving forward

This really is a "Do It Yourself book", just a casual flip through for a few minutes now and again will not suffice, you will end up saying "Oh, yes, I read Stop smoking for Good but it didn't help, patches are better for me." It is your activity, your involvement, your honesty and your questioning that will bring benefit to your life. The benefits are great, life is great. The more strength you use now doing this research and the more interest you show the better.

Also please don't be frightened by the exercises, they are very simple. Here is an example of one that you will be encouraged to do from time to time.

CLUTTER EXERCISE

Remove one piece of clutter from your house or garage, this can be a very small item, and if it has no value – pop it in the bin.

Just about everybody has something that has been lying around for a long time that needs removing even if it is an odd sock with a hole in it. Very easy, very effective and you can do it now.

When you have done it,

PUT A TICK IN THE BOX

And turn to the next page.

*   *   *   *   *

It is always the right time to do the right thing
(Michael Wilkey's Mother)

*   *   *   *   *

You might have noticed that some of your reasons you have listed for stopping come quite obviously from outside, for example it may be that your doctor or dentist have recommended or told you to stop. Other impulses have simply arisen from somewhere deep inside yourself, from your own volition and you say, "Yes, it is time for a big change, it's a natural step in my growth and self-development at this point in my life." Or you almost hear a voice saying "You are not invincible, you have been lucky, now is the time for you to stop." Try to make a distinction between these two types of reasons.

In days to come you will be able to look at your list and be absolutely sure, beyond a shadow of doubt, that you are doing the right thing in wanting to stop. Just as you are totally convinced that a square has more sides than a triangle you will be convinced that smoking is not a good activity for you and that stopping will improve every aspect of your life.

*   *   *   *   *

Not smoking can seriously improve the quality of your life.

*   *   *   *   *

LIST WRITTEN
    TICK IN THE BOX

And...   TURN
       THE
         PAGE

WOT NO LIST?

Please do not continue reading until you have taken the trouble to write your own list. A mental list is simply not sufficient; by writing with pen and paper you clarify your ideas and bring them down to earth strengthening your resolve and determination. It will be better to put the book away for another day or to try a different method rather than continue. You might well say," Look I am a mature professional person, I am too busy for doing research and writing out lists, those days are behind me, I have far better things to do with my time." (Smoke some more cigarettes?)

Respect the tick in a box system...... no tick..... no page turning!

PART TWO

FACING FACTS

"I must create a system of my own or become a slave to another person."
William Blake 1893

It really is a good thing that you have taken the trouble to create your list of reasons for stopping and this represents a positive and important step forward. It means that you have acknowledged that smoking is a problem and that you are prepared to do something about it. Hopefully you have left some space because there is more writing to be done later on!

By following the instructions step by step and doing the simple exercises you will develop enough will power and resolve to stop, and to stop for good. The more you put in at this stage the more you will take out later as you will have a longer, healthier and happier life.

Some readers may already be convinced that smoking is no longer for them and they have chosen to stub out their last cigarette. *

---

*Congratulations, great news, good decision, keep reading.

Others will say to themselves, "Yes, I can now see the situation more clearly; there is no doubt about it I have a mass of excellent reasons for stopping and not a single good reason to smoke. I certainly want to stop, I certainly should stop, but can I?"

The answer given here is, "Yes, an emphatic yes, you can stop for good, millions of people just like you have successfully done so."

Having your list is a positive and important step in the right direction, the next part of Wilkeys Plan is to make the transition from "wanting to stop" to "deciding to stop". These are two very separate stages and we will now take a look at different aspects of the smoking phenomena and find out how to make the decision to quit.

*   *   *   *   *

We will continue to look at smoking from as many different angles as possible and try to discover why people smoke and observe how they smoke. Just thinking about stopping is not sufficient, habits are deeply ingrained and you need to strongly "feel" the wish to stop before you can muster up sufficient "will" to do so. Keep your notebook handy and write as much about your quitting experience as possible, this is not only a "Do It Yourself" book, it is also a "Write It Yourself" book.

*   *   *   *   *

Take your time and do it right.
(Uncle Fred)

Readers will not all decide to stop at exactly the same moment; it is up to you when you stop, it is your life, your future and you are the person most affected. You have clear reasons and a strong motivation, you know that you should quit sometime and that you have no reason to continue smoking. Every aspect of your life will improve once you have stopped.

For some people the moment will suddenly come and they will be able to say "Yes, that's it, enough, I have finished!" others may prefer to work towards a specific date.

Which ever way you choose it will be a good thing at this point if you do the following:

Give up something you enjoy but that you know is not really good for you, anything. For example, stop eating chocolate or sugar or gambling and do it RIGHT NOW. You could choose to do without your morning cup of coffee or a glass of wine with dinner, select something that you KNOW you will be able to stop for at least three weeks. This will give you confidence that you have a fair measure of control over your life and when you know you can give up one thing its much easier to give up another.

Write in you notebook what it is that you are going to give up.

> *"I will commit myself to stopping* ....
>
> *for at least* .... *weeks from now* ....*"*

Written in notebook?

PUT A TICK IN THE BOX

This is one of several simple exercises given in the book, it takes no time at all and everybody is able to give up something for a few weeks. When the elected time has past you may well decide that you will leave it out of your life permanently. In our age fasting or Lent is not as widely practised as in early generations, this fostered a measure of self control and discipline that is perhaps missing today. Once again don't just say, "Oh yes, I can see that would be good for some people, but it's not necessary for me." Do it, and write in your note book that it is done. When you know how to stop one thing you know how to stop another.

＊　＊　＊　＊　＊

Everyday do something you don't want to do
and don't do something you do want to do.
(Michael Wilkey)

＊　＊　＊　＊　＊

It is notoriously difficult to encourage smokers to quit or even to suggest that they read a book such as this. Perhaps you are somewhat surprised to find yourself not only having read this far but also that you have made a list of your reasons for stopping, chucked out a piece of clutter and resolved to give up something for three weeks!

Because you have done all these things you should become

more and more aware that you are serious and can have a growing confidence that you will once again become a non-smoker. A non-smoker is someone who never smokes.

You are reading a book that tells you how to stop smoking, don't be tempted to just read on without doing the exercises saying, they are too easy. If they were too difficult or time consuming you would manage to use that as an excuse! This is a golden opportunity to tell yourself that the time has arrived to stop for good, you want to stop and you have many excellent reasons for doing so. You have the will power and know that your life will improve the moment you stop putting smoke into your lungs. The sooner you stop the better.

THE EFFECT OF NICOTINE
by Dr. Rudolf Steiner

Part of a discussion on 13th January 1923 in Switzerland when a question was raised concerning the effect of nicotine.
Published in *From Comets to Cocaine* by Rudolf Steiner Press, London.

Nicotine is a poison that is introduced into the human body through smoking and through tobacco in general. First, we must be clear how the effect of nicotine shows itself. The effect of nicotine shows itself above all in the activity of the heart. Through nicotine, an increased, stronger activity of the heart is called forth. The heart is not a pump, however, but only reflects what goes on in the body: the heart beats faster when the blood circulates faster. Nicotine therefore actually affects the blood circulation, animating it. One must therefore be clear that through the introduction of nicotine into the human body the blood circulation is stimulated. This, in turn, calls forth a stronger activity of the heart.

Now, this whole process in the human organism must be traced. You must be clear that everything occurring in the human organism is actually carefully regulated. One of the most important points regarding the human organism, for example, is the fact that the pulse rate of the adult is 72 beats a minute, and this holds true even into old age.

By comparison, as I have mentioned to you before, man takes about 18 breaths a minute. When you multiply 18 x 4, you get 72. This means that on average the blood substance pulses four times as quickly through the body as does the breath. Of course, these are average figures; they differ slightly in each human being. The fact that this ratio varies in people accounts for the differences between them, but on average it is 1:4; that is, the blood circulation is four times more intense than that of the breathing rhythm.

Part Two: Change and Growth

If I now introduce nicotine into the human organism, I can do it for two reasons – first, because of a strong liking for tobacco, and second, as a remedy. Every substance that is poisonous is also a remedy. Everything, one can say, is both poisonous and healing. If, for example, you drink several buckets of water, they naturally have a poisonous effect, whereas the proper amount is a means of sustenance, and when it is introduced in unusually small amounts, it can even be a remedy. As a matter of fact, water is generally a potent remedy when certain methods are employed. It can therefore be said that even the most commonplace substances can be poisons as well as remedies. This is why the effect that a given substance has on the human organism must be known.

If I introduce tobacco into the human organism, it first stimulates the blood circulation. The blood becomes more active, circulating more vigorously. Breathing, however, is not stimulated to the same degree by tobacco; the breathing rhythm remains the same. The blood circulation is therefore no longer synchronized with the breathing. When people introduce nicotine into their bodies, they really need a blood circulation different from the one they normally have.

Let us, for example, imagine someone whose system was adjusted to the exact average of 18 breaths and 72 pulse beats (there aren't any such people, but let's assume it). Now, nicotine causes his pulse rate to increase to, let us say 76 beats. The correct ratio between pulse and respiration is thus altered. The result is that the blood doesn't receive enough oxygen, since a certain amount is supposed to be absorbed into the blood with each pulse beat. The consequence of nicotine poisoning, therefore, is that the blood demands too much oxygen. The breathing process does not supply enough oxygen, and a slight shortness of breath occurs. This shortness of breath is, of course, so negligible that it escapes notice; after all, as I have told you, the human body can take a lot of abuse.

Nevertheless, the use of nicotine always calls forth a definite, very slight shortness of breath. This slight shortness of breath causes with each breath a feeling of anxiety. Every shortness of breath causes a feeling of anxiety. It is easier to control a normal sensation of anxiety than this terrible slight anxiety, of which one is completely unconscious. When something like anxiety, fear, or shock remains unnoticed, it is a direct source of illness.

Such a source of illness is constantly present in a person who is a heavy smoker because, without realizing it, he is always filled with a certain anxiety. Now, you know that if you suffer from anxiety, your heart pumps more quickly. This leads you to realize that the heart of a person who constantly poisons himself with nicotine continuously beats somewhat too fast. When it beats too quickly, however the heart thickens, just as the muscle of the upper arm, the biceps, grow thicker when it is constantly strained. Under some circumstances, this is not so bad, as long as the inner tissue doesn't tear, If the heart muscle - it is also a muscle - becomes too thick from overexertion, however, it exerts pressure on all the other organs with the result, as a rule, that beginning from the heart the blood circulation becomes disturbed. The circulation of the blood cannot be initiated by the heart, but it can be disturbed when the heart is thickened.

The next consequence of a thickened heart is that the kidneys become ill, since it is due to the harmonious activities of heart and kidneys that the entire human bodily organization is kept functioning properly. The heart and kidneys must always work in harmony. Naturally, everything in the human being must harmonize, but the heart and kidneys are directly connected. It quickly becomes apparent that when something is amiss in the heart, the kidneys no longer function properly. Urinary elimination no longer works in the right way with the result that man develops a much too rapid tempo of life and comes to wear himself out too quickly. A person who takes into his body too much nicotine in relation to his bodily proportions therefore will slowly but surely deteriorate. Actually, he gradually perishes from a variety of inner conditions of anxiety that influence the heart.

The effects of states of anxiety on the activities of the soul can easily be determined. In people who have introduced too much nicotine into their bodies, it becomes noticeable that gradually their power of thought is also impaired. The power of thought is impaired, because man can no longer think properly when he lives in anxiety. Nicotine poisoning, therefore, can be recognized by the fact that such peoples thoughts are no longer quite in order. They usually jump to conclusions much too quickly. They sometimes intensify this overly rapid judgement to paranoid thoughts. We can therefore say that the use of nicotine for pleasure actually undermines human health.

In all such matters, however, you must consider the other side. Smoking is something that has only come about in humanity's recent evolution. Originally, human beings did not smoke, and it is only recently that the use of tobacco has become fashionable. Now let us look at the other side of the coin.

Let us assume that a persons pulse beats only 68 instead of 72 times per minute. Such a person, whose blood circulation is not animated enough, now begins to smoke. You see, then his blood circulation is stimulated in the right direction, from 68 to 72, so that his blood circulation and breathing harmonize. If, therefore, a doctor notices that an illness is caused by weak blood circulation, he may even advise his patient to smoke.

FACING MORE FACTS

This is a little exercise you can do that has a look at the smoking phenomena, its easy, it is in two parts and it's optional! Some people are tempted to say I will not do these exercises because they are all too simple, they can not possibly work. The only way to find out is to do them just as the only way to learn how to ride a bicycle is to try.

OUTSIDE OBSERVER

Part 1

Go into a bar or café where groups of people are smoking, take a seat and observe everyone around you as if you were a journalist or detective. The idea is not to criticize but to look as carefully as possible at everything and everyone and find out exactly what is going on and use all your senses. You will notice things such as the following: men and women of different ages sit round a table each with a brightly coloured packet of cigarettes and a cigarette lighter, some of them very expensive. Almost automatically they pass each other cigarettes and light them; this seems to play a big part in the smoking process turning it into a kind of ritual. Their smoking actions appear to be ingrained and habitual, and they sometimes try to avoid blowing smoke in each others' faces. Women seem to behave a little differently from men, they try harder to avoid smoke getting into their eyes and nose, and they don't inhale so deeply, they tend to extinguish the cigarette when only half smoked. From time to time a waiter empties the ashtray and replaces it with a clean one, etc.

Once you have quietly observed for a while try to imagine what the people are feeling. How much enjoyment are they getting? What is it doing for them? Are they happier and more satisfied when they have finished and stubbed out the cigarette than before, or are they thinking, "Good, that's the end of that?"

Have little thoughts such as, "None of these people would normally want to harm themselves, so why are they choosing to introduce tars and nicotine into their bodies?" "If they like each other why are they blowing second hand smoke into each others' faces?"

Which words would best describe their activity? Happy, discontent, satisfied, nervous, pleased, aware, etc.

Part 2

At home when you have a quiet five minutes, sit down and recreate the scene in your imagination, perhaps adding your-self to the group of smokers. Imagine this from somewhere outside, again not judgementally, simply observe.

* * * * *

This exercise can be extended by imagining the whole episode (or a book or play) in reverse sequence. Of course, it requires constant practice, but can help to overcome nerv-ousness and lead to an improvement of memory. During the restless daily bustle, it is hard to find the inner quiet that such exercises require, and in the evening one is too tired, but the rewards make the effort worthwhile. If you took the trouble to do this exercise, write an account of it in your notebook – the more involved you become by writing down your experiences, the better.

* * * * *

It is your job to convince yourself that cigarettes are no longer going to be part of your life, and that you will be far better off without them. You are the person best able and equipped to discover reasons for stopping; it is your life and your responsibility.

You might still be in the position where you can trick yourself into believing there is something good about smoking. You might say that it relieves pain and stress of life, that it helps you relax, that it helps you concentrate, that it is social, etc. Look carefully at these excuses and you will see that they are contradictory and untrue – one cigarette makes you want another, they cause pain and stress. They don't make you relax, they excite and increase your blood pressure, they are anti-social and divisive. Tobacco companies want to keep you hooked and tell you that "cigarettes relax you", etc., and it is only when you have stopped smoking will you be able to fully see through what is happening. This is the nature of drugs – everybody can put up strong arguments for their drug of choice on an "I would rather have my drug than yours" basis. Stopping will be difficult for people who can consider that there is something beneficial about smoking. You have to convince yourself that there is absolutely nothing good about smoking. Absolutely nothing.

You have clear reasons and a strong motivation to stop and you know that you should quit sometime, you have no reason to continue and from the moment that you stop both your health and the quality of your life will improve. The time to "stop for good" is coming closer and this should become something to look forward to as it will enhance the rest of your life. You will be releasing yourself from self imposed slavery and taking off the ball and chain from your own leg; that has got to be sensible and good. Just cutting down is not sufficient, by stopping you will be moving from an unnatural state back to a natural one because we all started out as non-smokers.

*   *   *   *   *

Here is another optional exercise.

AWARENESS

Perform one series of actions each day where you become "as aware" as possible of each of your movements. This can be simply walking slowly for a short distance, and as you do so, you observe the "lifting" and "carrying" and "placing" of first one foot and then the other. Do this for twenty or so paces. (Of course concentrating on each part of each step is far, far from simple and requires constant practise!). Or you can make a cup of tea, speaking to yourself all the while: "I am now pouring boiling water into a small tea pot, I am now placing the lid on the pot... etc." Again, far from simple, but very effective.

Feel free to put this in your notebook and resolve to do it each day for the next few weeks.

THINGS SMOKERS SAY AND DO NOT SAY

"I can stop smoking any time I like."

"I have stopped hundreds of times."

"I don't want to stop."

"I am fully aware that cigarettes are expensive and don't need you or any book to tell me that I am paying to kill myself."

"Smoking is one of my great pleasures."

"I really look forward to having a cigarette."

"People who have stopped are the worst naggers."

"I must stop soon, I am killing myself."

"Smoking only harms me, it is entirely my own concern."

"If I stop I will put on weight."

"I smoke because otherwise people will think I am too pure."

"I don't like it, it burns my mouth"

"Oh, I really enjoyed that cigarette."

"I like standing near bonfires and car exhausts."

"Every time I have a cigarette it makes me want another one."

Part Two: Change and Growth

"I see the price of cigs has gone up again."

"What health warning?"

"I have cut down a lot."

"I can stop but it makes me bad tempered and I can't concentrate."

"I only smoke five cigarettes a day because I don't like them very much."

"I am fully aware that cigarettes are bad for my health and don't need you or any book to tell me."

"I am fully aware that I have been brain washed into smoking and don't need you or any book to tell me."

"Certainly cigarette smoking has become much less socially acceptable recently but I am free to smoke, smoking is a human right."

"Yes, smoking is a silly thing to do, nicotine is very addictive and certainly the best thing is never to start."

"Cigarettes kill me so slowly that I hardly notice."

"I will stop one day."

"I will stop someday."

"I will stop when.........."

"I would find it impossible to give a child any good reason

why I smoke and would certainly suggest that they never start. People under 21 shouldn't be allowed to buy cigarettes."

"I only smoke cigars."

"I have a dreadful problem; I am hooked on the wretched things. I have spent a fortune on patches, they work but the moment I stop using them I need cigarettes again."

"I still smoke even though my doctor told me to quit."

"Smoking is the worst thing I do, I would be really proud of myself if I stopped."

*   *   *   *   *

Another task for you; add at least two more things to this list that you have heard people say and one you have said yourself. Write them in your notebook and leave room for more as you come across them.

PUT A TICK IN THE BOX

THE DECISION TO STOP

Is it difficult for you to live the life of a monk?
No, not at all. Deciding to become a monk was difficult.
(A. Monk)

* * * * *

For many people "deciding to stop" is more difficult than actually stopping.

This may seem like a very strange thing to say but take a moment to think about what is happening. Stopping is a massive decision, no matter how good your reasons, and only a smoker can know just what a huge decision it is. Before each of life's big decision, for example marriage, a time is usually put aside for reflection which proceeds the actual "moment" of decision. This is the "moment" of choice, the "moment" of freedom, once the decision has been made a new life, for better or for worse, begins and there is now an end to doubt. Doubts vanish, it is beyond question.

In the case of smoking you can be absolutely sure that the decision to stop will lead to a better life opening up before you. The reason for putting off the decision is fear, fear of pain, fear of failure or fear of change. Be clear, smoking is not natural; change is natural, it requires courage and leads to growth.

Realising that you have a problem with smoking and dispelling as many illusions as possible represents a big step forward and in some ways you have already done the hard part. A half hearted decision will not carry you far, you want to be fully committed so that you quit once and for all, for good. A life free from dependence on nicotine is something to look forward to.

*   *   *   *   *

Try this if you are still smoking:

Change your brand of cigarettes to ones that you don't like.

CHANGE

Life is a continuous process of transformation whereby we encounter ourselves; we encounter what we wish to become and also what resists being transformed. Change involves a certain amount of pain as we move from a position of comfort or "stuckness" into a new situation. Change is the one sure thing in life. We all have something to learn and thresholds to cross, for the moment ours is to stop smoking but it could equally well be one of a thousand different things, eating too much, gossip, meanness, too much TV, impulsive shopping, idleness, greed, jealousy, the list is endless.

It might be that earlier when reading about how the cigarette companies have conned and manipulated millions of people into smoking you felt a little bit angry and were tempted to shift at least some of the blame for your predicament onto them. This is understandable and has some justification but is something that you will have to see through. Certainly you were younger then and more vulnerable to their sneaky tricks but now you know better and you are not going to condemn yourself to a life of being a victim. It might be that you grew up in a house where smoking was seen as a harmless social activity, well now you know better and you can not pass the blame onto other people all your life. Right now you have a good opportunity to become "unstuck", to do something about it, millions of people have already successfully stopped and you can join them.

Nicotine and packets of cigarettes have absolutely no problem, they really don't care whether you smoke or not but it does makes an enormous difference to you, it is your problem, your responsibility and it is for you to come up with the solution. The solution is to stop and the result will be a happier, healthier, longer active life.

Why is smoking such a fascinating subject? A more correct title for this book would be, "How can "I" stop "myself" smoking, for good?" The subject is YOU, your health, desires, cravings, wishes, hopes, ideals, fears, thoughts, courage and freedom, that's why it's fascinating and why it's worth spending time on. Life offers us many diversions and we can become so busy that we can avoid ever looking at ourselves. Perhaps this is the one good thing that can be said about nicotine, it can encourage us to take a good look at ourselves to find out what is going on, to ask questions such as; "How can I balance what I "want" to do and what I "ought" to do." - "What should I do with my desires and wishes? Shall I control them, transform them, indulge them or ignore them?" - "Why do I do the things I shouldn't and don't do the things I should?" etc.

Something has come along in your life and initiated a desire for change, perhaps it is coming quite obviously from outside, a family member has become sick from smoking or there has been another price increase. Perhaps more mysteriously it comes from somewhere inside, a little voice saying "Be careful, you have been very lucky so far but you are not invincible, now is the time to stop. Wake up, there is no smoke without fire."

For some reason you have decided to seriously read a "How to stop smoking book" and are doing some thinking and getting deeply involved in the subject. It might be a question of your age, it is said that life develops in seven year cycles, or you have become aware that you have given your body a battering over the years and waking up to the fact that you are not immortal.

You may well be thinking;

"What happens if I add on ten or twenty years to my present age, will I really still be smoking?"

"It is certainly better to stop before the doctor tells me that I must."

"When will I actually stop smoking instead of just continually kidding myself that I am going to? Is this a now or never moment?"

It might be because of pregnancy or the chance of pregnancy, it might be because you have learnt of someone suffering form the obvious effects of smoking or any one of a hundred different reasons. A turning point has certainly arrived and perhaps you can work out why. Don't worry if you can't, just be thankful for it, take it seriously and grasp the wonderful opportunity.

We can busy ourselves from morning to night with life's distractions, sport, making money, etc, and avoid ever having an honest look at ourselves. This could be a good time for you to sit down quietly and have a complete review of your biography and while you do so you might discover that stopping smoking is not the only important change that you would like to make to your life.

*　　*　　*　　*　　*

Time to do this one again.

CHUCK OUT ONE PIECE OF CLUTTER

Most people can find a piece of clutter without too much difficulty, if it doesn't have any value pick it up and pop it in the bin. This precipitates a little change, a decision, a little act of will and it makes a space for something new to come into your life. You might think that such a small thing won't make any difference but that's not so, it does. It really is not difficult, you are not being asked to empty the garage, and it doesn't take long. Decide for yourself how much and how often you want to rid yourself of unnecessary things that have been lying around for months or years on end. The more you can find the better.

Have you actually DONE that?

This is something for you to DO and just reading about it is a waste of time. You can buy a "How to play guitar" book, but until you start to do the exercises you will not make progress.

TICK IN THE BOX (before moving to the next page)

IT'S ALL ABOUT HEALTH*

The time is always right to make some improvements in both our eating habits and how much exercise we take. Now is an ideal opportunity to take some steps in this direction. It will make you more health aware, as a smoker this aspect of your life might well have been neglected and something that you were reluctant to look at closely. Health is a most serious business and even more important than wealth, the more health conscious you become the more reluctant you will be to allow tars and nicotine into your body. Your health will improve dramatically from the moment you decide to stop, you will look better and feel fitter.

Medical advisors are repeatedly encouraging us to:

- Eat more fresh fruit and vegetables and have a sensible junk free low fat, low salt and low sugar diet.

- Exercise for at least an hour every day, preferably in the fresh air on foot or bicycle.

- Avoid stressful situations and practice some kind of relaxation or meditation.

- Cut down on tea, coffee, and alcohol.

We know that this is good advice and it's entirely up to each of us to take some action and this means educating ourselves, experimenting and finding out what's right for us. Our health is our responsibility and not something that can be

---

*Health Warning: In the interest of good health it is always important to consult your doctor before commencing any diet or exercise programme.

passed onto another person. The same medical advisors will almost certainly say "The single biggest improvement that can be made to health is to stop smoking".

Take your notebook and a pen and map out a daily "keep fit" programme to cover at least the next three weeks, it should represent a significant improvement to your present fitness regime. It doesn't have to be a dramatic marathon training programme and the most important thing is that you make your plan and keep to it. Be realistic, because it is very important at this stage that you complete all the tasks that you set yourself. Not only will your health improve, but you willpower and self-confidence will also increase.

Three headings are needed:

DIET

For some of us the extent of our nutritional knowledge is being told to "eat up your carrots" as children. Now is a good time for you to look further into discovering the diet that is right for you, it is your life and there is an abundance of nutritional advice out there so do start making some enquiries and experiments. Simply moving towards eating wholemeal bread, more fresh fruit and vegetables and cutting down on fats and sugar will make a big difference. Even if you write "I will eat one extra piece of fruit each day" that's fine, but DO IT.

PHYSICAL EXERCISE

With exercise it's the same story so have a look around and you will discover that there is something out there for you, it could be walking, swimming, jogging, karate, squash or dance, the list is endless. Doctors recommend that most people take at least an hour of light exercise each day.

STRESS REMOVAL

Stress can be removed by changes in lifestyle using such things as yoga, meditation, reading poetry, and making sure that you eat regular meals slowly in a quiet environment. Here again there are so many wonderful things available but it is up to you to find the right thing. Simply avoiding some situations such as listening to the gloomy news too frequently, driving fast, being in a hurry generally and watching violent films will be of great benefit.

The exercises given in this book provide a good foundation for improving health generally and they can bring control and balance into your life Constant practise is more important than trying for quick results.

It will also be an enormous value if you are able to establish a daily rhythm for at least three weeks from the date you stop smoking. This will ideally mean rising at the same time, having regular family meals, and going to bed at the same time (preferably before 11.00pm), it is one of the most important aids that can be introduced to your life as it brings strength of resolve and will make stopping easier. A natural rhythm is not the same as a routine; the sun rises at a slightly different time each day.

Once you stop smoking, physical exercise will act as a positive reinforcement for your decision and be an outlet for increased energy. It is most unlikely that you will want to smoke after jogging, swimming or a game of tennis as they don't mix well together.

Your lifestyle will almost certainly not be as calm and peaceful as it is for the monk in his monastery; our modern world is simply not like that. The world is incredibly noisy; we are bombarded by advertising and are constantly being urged to go faster and consume more. The answer is to create a few minutes now and again to take the rush out of life, to use moments to make quiet observations while waiting for the late train rather than getting stressed out. Easy to say but it is good to try and it is the attempt that counts. What we are given or have is not as important as what we can achieve; even the snake must shed its skin in order to grow.

Have you written out your new health programme? Did you include a section about bringing more rhythm into your life?

Good, then put a

TICK IN THE BOX

*   *   *   *   *

There is not much point in living if you are
not prepared to change.
(Aunt Agnes)

PRIMING THE PUMP

These days most people get through life without ever having the experience of priming a water pump. The trick used to be to pour a small quantity of water into the pump to displace air and thus promote suction. To stop smoking requires an initial effort and afterwards you are rewarded with an increase in energy. The more effort you put into writing in your note book, doing research and generally becoming involved in the process the easier it will be to quit for good. Review all you have written so far and feel sure that you have done your best and really primed the pump; time spent now will result in the liberation of much more energy and increase your confidence. What you are doing now will effect the rest of your life.

Have another look too at your reasons for wanting to stop, they provide excellent motivation and the time is approaching to actually quit. Here are some suggestions as to how you can prepare for the moment.

1. Don't worry it will be an anti climax its so easy.

2. Find a time when you are geographically stable and can establish a daily rhythm for at least a week and preferably much longer

3. Think about going on a fast for the first three days.*

---

*For some people it is definitely worth considering a complete fast for three days or even a week to coincide with stopping. During this time pangs for nicotine become confused with feeling peckish as they are very similar, there is a wealth of information available about fasting and it is not very difficult to stop eating for a few days as you can allow yourself food

4. Make some other change right now, for example stop eating chocolate or drinking coffee. Cut out alcohol for the first few weeks after stopping as it can weaken your will and diminish resolve.

5. Buy a good stock of fresh vegetables, fruits and pure water. Look out for "organic" or "bio-dynamic" foods which are chemical free.

6. Activate your plan for increasing exercise both daily and weekly.

7. Make up your mind not to use patches, gums, or substitute tobaccos.

8. Do not wait for the perfect moment, life always has its ups and downs.

9. Being a non-smoker is something to look forward to, it will affect every aspect of your life and you will become a stronger person.

*   *   *   *   *

*There is nothing to worry about in stopping;
it is people who keep smoking that are the ones with
a problem.*

*   *   *   *   *

---

supplements and fruit juices. There is no fear of putting on weight when you are fasting! When you start eating again there may well be some items, such as coffee, that you will wish to eliminate permanently and with a new start you can try out a new diet.

We have looked long enough at the problem of nicotine addiction and the moment has now arrived to stop. Stop does mean stop, completely. The idea of smoking in moderation, of cutting down has to be forgotten, one cigarette leads to the next. It would mean that you are stopping several times a day, a perpetual torture that for most people is virtually impossible. Ask an occasional smoker why they don't stop completely and they will have to invent a very a strange answer. Smoking is not a pleasure, it's a nuisance.

Don't fall into the trap of using gums or patches, at best they only offer a substitute and with the simple exercises given here are just not necessary – save your money and have trust in your own determination. Gums act in the same way as cigarettes in activating saliva and your stomach thinks wrongly that it is going to receive some food. The point of this book is that you are stopping because it is your own decision and you're doing it out of your own strength. You only stop once, for good.

There will never be a perfect moment; life will always provide little tests and moments of stress. It's up to you to pick the time and tell yourself to stop; a book can't do that for you. When you have stubbed out your last cigarette turn the page, you have definitely made the right decision; you have changed your life and become a non smoker. You don't want any more, you don't need anymore, it's a great feeling.

* * * * *

If you have decided to stop FOR GOOD turn the page and discover just what a wonderful decision you have made. Remember it was a free decision and one that you will be given the confidence and strength to handle.

YOU ARE DOING THE RIGHT THING
FOR THE RIGHT REASON

*   *   *   *   *

I AM QUITE SURE I DON'T WANT TO SMOKE
ANYMORE AND HAVE DECIDED TO QUIT.

Date.......................

.............Turn the page...............

Go on.

I AM UNDECIDED

If you haven't decided to stop just yet don't worry, put the book away for now and start it again from the beginning another day. By reading this far you have prepared fertile ground and sown some seeds which need time to germinate. Stopping will not be far away, you have wonderful motivation and just need a bit more time to muster up the courage to stop. When you do tell yourself to stop it will be much easier than you think, the exercises (take a peep at the ones still to come) will give great support so keep on with them and the health programme.

BEGIN IT NOW

Begin it now!
Until one is committed, there is hesitancy,
the chance to draw back, always ineffectiveness.
Concerning all acts of initiative (and creation),
there is one elementary truth, the ignorance of which
kills countless ideas and splendid plans:
That the moment one definitely commits oneself,
then Providence moves too.
All sorts of things occur to help one
that would never otherwise have occurred.
A whole stream of events issues from the decision,
raising in one's favour all manner of unforeseen incidents
and meetings and material assistance, which no man
could have dreamed would have come his way.
Whatever you can do, or dream you can, begin it.
Boldness has Genius, Power and Magic in it.
Begin it now!

Johann Wolfgang Goethe

PART THREE

CONGRATULATIONS

YOU ARE A NON-SMOKER,

YOU HAVE REVERTED TO A NATURAL STATE

The first step will be to clear out all traces of your old habit. Every cigarette packet, all matches, lighters, ashtrays, the whole lot... take them all for a walk and say goodbye and good riddance. They are no longer required.

Take a shower, clean your teeth, put on clean clothes and begin to feel better.

YOU HAVE DEFINITELY MADE THE RIGHT DECISION, you have not lost anything only gained.

Treat yourself to a bunch of beautiful fresh cut flowers, arrange them in a vase, perhaps where the ashtray used to be, and realize what a wonderful improvement you have made to your life.

Welcome to a longer, healthier life.

Now pick up your notebook and re-read your reasons for wanting to stop.

THEY ARE ALL EXCELLENT REASONS, each one of them taken alone would give sufficient incentive to quit; together they become an unstoppable force.

Stopping really is very easy and it becomes easier by the day. The task now is to reinforce your decision and this book provides simple exercises that will help you break the habit and increase your will power to make sure that you do not to start again.

Just reading about the exercises is not enough, they need to be done, they are incredibly simple and they are incredibly effective. Here is one you can do straight away.

Sit down quietly with your notebook and pen,

And write:

"IT REALLY FEELS WONDERFUL TO BE FREE FROM SMOKE AND NICOTINE"

But, do this left handed and write it out at least three times*.

The sentence chosen is simply an example which you can use or you can invent one of your own. (e.g. "I no longer need to smoke and have no desire to do so") Write out the same sentence everyday at the same time if you can, you might care to use it first thing in the morning and last thing at night

---

*Of course right handed if you are left handed!

or if you feel like a cigarette. Keep some pages free for this daily exercise.

Don't look for miracles, your life is sure to improve, be realistic and don't expect too much too quickly, in a word take it easy, have patience, its wonderful stuff. Do this exercise everyday and don't dismiss it as "too easy".

Heading in notebook:

DAILY EXERCISE No 1
Write a sentence three times left handed.

TICK IN THE BOX

LIFE AS A NON-SMOKER

Your life has changed, or better said you have changed your own life by your own endeavour which is why it was suggested that you stop without pills, medicines, patches or gums. Next time you see your doctor tell her you have stopped, she will be pleased and supportive and may provide suggestions for diet and exercise. Certainly acupuncturists, hypnotists, councillors, homeopaths, Chinese medicines and therapists have their place and their successes but this way you know that its 100% because of your own efforts and this will give you an increased confidence that you will not relapse. Not only will you have stopped smoking but you will rightly have a growing sense of self esteem and gradually realize that you have the strength to pass other thresholds. You can also be sure that the quality of your life will improve.

It is time for you to do some more writing.

Open your notebook and read through

"My reasons to stop smoking"

before beginning another list called:

"My reasons for not starting again"

The more positive reasons you can think up the better because this will anchor and reinforce your decision. You might think that reasons for stopping and reasons for not starting are exactly the same, they may well be similar but this is a different stage in the process and it is very necessary to have this second list.

Please be sure to write down that you do not have a single reason to start again and that there is absolutely nothing to be gained from smoking.

TICK IN THE BOX

CHECK LIST

Your note book should now include the following;

1.   Reasons for wanting to stop

2.   Exercise and diet plan

3.   Chuck out clutter

4.   I have stopped.................for three weeks from...................

5.   I stopped smoking for good on ....

6.   Daily exercise No 1, write a sentence left hand-ed

7.   Reasons for not starting again.

Keep a note of all your experiences and you could even have a whole section called "How I stopped smoking"

THE NEIGHBOUR

John Davidson lived in one of the fourth floor bed-sits and was 69 years of age when I first met him. Once this had been a grand house in a grand part of town but now was divided into accommodation for people best described as poor. The attic floor had housed the servants of slave traders and was reached by a steep narrow wooden staircase giving access to four bed-sits with windows cut into the low angled roof allowing views of the sky. Each of the tiny apartments had a door leading onto the dark airless landing which had been painted a shade of Thames blue. Much of the paint had peeled to reveal a previous layer of brown.

A month after moving in I was able to establish a nodding acquaintance with my three neighbours, an Irishman who had the largest flat, a German widow who had at least three cats and, John who lived directly opposite me. The idea seemed to be that we keep ourselves to ourselves and this arrangement suited me just fine. I had recently made a fool of myself in another city and had decided to run away and cover myself in work and study. It is what they call "a long story" or "the stuff of life". I don't know where this expression originated but it is certainly not the one you wish to hear when you are right in the middle of it. My days were filled with earning enough money to pay the rent and my evenings with classes of further education which became less and less interesting. The nights were unsuccessfully spent trying to forget and forgive.

In my room, overcrowded with tasteless furniture, for some reason there were four chairs, I had sufficient space for a sagging bed, to wash and prepare one-pot meals on a little electric cooker called a "Baby Belling". Mr. Belling had carefully designed this apparatus for rooms the size of mine and had been thoughtful enough to provide an oven just large enough for two pies. Hot water and all electrical appliances, the baby Belling and a two bar electric heater, required coins to be inserted into a meter almost continually.

Life suited me pretty well, work was totally undemanding and I had committed myself to two years of study for the first time since leaving school, the subjects were absorbing but the teaching methods something of a bore. I was able to borrow books from the student library and would read several each week. Diverging thus from the strict curriculum I managed to keep myself amused. Happy to be alone with my own miserable melancholy I fitted very well into the spirit of the household.

Of my fellow neighbours it was John who I encountered most frequently, and we exchanged the time of day on our little landing. He had the unmistakable air of a bachelor, and there were plenty of clues to indicate that he managed to live without an iron or ever visiting a dry cleaner. Often there were tufted areas of grey hair that he had missed while shaving on his lower chin, close to his ear and just below his nose. No one was available or intimate enough with him to point this out. I can imagine that he had been very handsome as a young man, with an erect strong bearing that had become over time a kind of stoop with his neck and head permanently protruding forwards. He walked, or shuffled, with the aid of a stick while somehow maintaining the bearing of a military campaigner – one or two medals dangling from his tweed jacket would not have been out of place.

Perhaps every other month he visited a hairdresser, and for a few days had an even parting on the left side of his head, this soon disappeared leaving a tangle of grey and white hairs. It was with some difficulty and many pauses that he climbed the four flights of stairs to our landing, and I often found myself stuck behind him. I felt somewhat awkward squeezing past to dash ahead of him, and invariably I offered to carry his little brown bag, containing the shopping he had purchased at the corner store, up the remaining flights of stairs. The faded canvas bag had a single strap by which it hung from his right shoulder crossing his chest and enabled him to carry his supplies and keep both hands free. In his left hand he had a walking stick and with his right he could grip the banister rail and move slowly from landing to landing by placing first his right foot on a step and then his left.

He spoke softly and slowly with traces of a Northern accent that he either tried to conceal or that had been worn away by time. After five or six such meetings he invited me for tea in his room. I think I was the first visitor he had received for several months or possibly years. His bedsit, like mine was over cluttered with shabby furniture, leaving very little floor space. I found a spot to put his bag of shopping on the small sink while he found a teapot, cups and saucers, and even a little blue and white striped jug for milk from the back of a cupboard. When the metal kettle had boiled it blew steam through a whistle attachment on the spout. We sat at either end of his little table that was sensibly covered with a well-worn blue plastic sheet, and waited for the tea to brew.

I soon found myself in a one way conversation by telling him about my life, my attempts to study and something of my plans for the future without learning anything about him. He reminded me of the Caretaker in Pinter's play who was always off to Sidcup to collect "some papers" which did or didn't exist. I had the clear impression that either Pinter himself or the actor I had seen portraying the character had actually met John.

After the tea had "mashed" and we had drunk our first cup we began to speak of our neighbours. As John had lived here for six years he was able to contribute much more information than me. The Irishman, he said, had a beautiful flat, very large with two windows on the sunny side of the house, but he got more noise from the traffic. It seems that two young girls had lived in my flat before me, but "they didn't quite fit in", and the landlord asked them to leave. He was able to tell me a little about the German widow who I had hardly seen, and I learnt that she had been here for twelve years and was related to the landlord in some way; John estimated the cat population in her room to be four or five.

He was reticent to tell me much about his own life on this occasion, but said that he was happy enough and spent much of his time in the library, particularly in winter, and in the park during summer. Each Christmas all the people who lived on the top floor were invited by the Irishman into his flat and had a wonderful Christmas dinner and some drinks. He said he would like to find a downstairs flat, but they were much bigger and far too expensive. When he was too old and "crotchety" to walk upstairs he supposed that he would be re-housed by the council and put into a home.

"I will hang on here for as long as I can, I think I'm good for a few more years, I don't want to be a burden on the state. I had a fall ten years ago and now I have arthritis and lumbago, really I should go somewhere warm to live but need to stay on here for at least another month or so and finish a few things off."

His room was mostly filled by a single bed and four chairs, but in one corner under the skylight there was a table housing an old-fashioned ribbon typewriter and on either side of it folders containing reams of papers. I had often heard the sound of typing coming from his room as I walked past his door both during the day and sometimes at night. It was a very slow methodical one or two finger tap, tap, tap, followed by a crunching sound and a bell as the carriage was moved to begin a new line. This activity would sometimes continue for several hours and had often aroused my curiosity, as I could not think what on earth could be occupying so much of his time.

While we drank our tea together I told him that I was always happy and available to help with shopping, and said he was welcome to come over and see me at any time. On leaving I suggested that he come round on Sunday for lunch, and we could have a little meal together. He thought this was a good idea.

The following Sunday morning when I went shopping for the newspaper I purchased an extra pie, but was unsure if John would either remember or care to visit. At about 12.30 pm there was a knock on the door and John was standing outside with quite a beam on his face.

"Come in John and sit down. I need some time to get everything ready and you can read the Sunday paper while I'm cooking." Clearly Mr Belling had planned for such occasions and I was able for the first time to fill the little oven and use the two heating rings to full capacity.

John didn't speak as I endeavoured to cook mashed potatoes, mixed vegetables and gravy; this was quite an ambitious and delicate operation, but I even managed to warm the plates. I glanced at John from time to time and saw that he was engrossed with the large Sunday paper and all its supplements, and seemed to be reading it in its entirety. As I brought the plates and food to the table I explained that this was the first time I had cooked for two in my flat. He took a great interest and enjoyment in his meal and spoke little as he ate. I had the impression that such a lunch was a rare occasion for him and he seemed to eat everything as though he were tasting it for the first time.

When we had finished and were sitting with cups of coffee at the table with plates and pots in the sink, he looked around the room and said, "The trade was triangular apparently. Trinkets, alcohol, cloth on the Outward Passage, to pay for the merchandise of course. The actual cargo was branded and stowed for the Middle Passage. Like sardines. It must have been horrible for them I imagine. On the Return Passage the ships brought rum and molasses back to England. I'm sorry, living alone in this house... my mind wanders some times." I thought it best to say nothing. Then he picked up the travel section of the paper and asked if I had seen an article about two English girls who had gone to Belize to work as teachers for six months. I told him that I had not read the piece which he passed to me, and as I was glancing through it he said, "That's where I'm going, Belize, they speak English and it will be nice and hot."

This sounded rather unlikely for a man in his seventies, and I thought he had no idea of the enormous distance involved perhaps confusing it with somewhere fifty miles away. Rather than pursue the matter I thought it wise to try to change the subject by asking him what he had been doing that morning.

"On Sunday mornings I go to the churchyard, that's where I have my little job. After the funerals are well and truly over I collect all the old wreathes and clean them up, take all the old flowers off and give the wire a bit of a polish. First thing Monday morning I take them round to the florist, who gives me a little bit of money and then uses them again. I suppose you could say I am in the recycling business, but with my small pension it means I have a few bob for extras. Some people might think its a bit morbid, but I wanted to save up for my own funeral. I have been doing it for years and now I will use my savings for a passage to Belize, how much do you think the fare will be for the ship or is it better to go with a plane?"

My attempt to change the subject hadn't really succeeded and I looked at airfares in the travel section of the newspaper. "I think you would have to fly all the way to Mexico and then take a bus for a few days through Guatemala, the fare works out at about £600 return. You know it's a very, very long way."

"Oh no I don't want a return, it will be instead of moving to an old folk's home. I have got at least seven hundred pounds in my Post Office savings. Next week I will go and get a passport and buy a ticket".

"What are you going to do with all your things?" I asked

him half entering into the spirit of the idea and half humouring him.

"Well now I'm just going down to pay my rent and give the landlord two weeks notice. I haven't got so many things, just bits and pieces I got from jumble sales. I will take my umbrella and a towel with me and take everything else down to the charity shops if they will have them. Do you want to have a typewriter? It works very well and I don't need it any more because I've finished."

It was dawning on me that that I was in the presence of a very sweet but nevertheless rambling old man.

"What else do you think I should take, my umbrella, a towel, it will be very hot won't it?"

"Yes, it will certainly be very, very hot; I should think a hat would be a good idea."

"Oh yes a hat, I have got a trilby and a cheese cloth cap, they would do nicely. Do you think I could use my pensioners pass on the bus in Mexico?"

Now I thought his fantasy had gone far enough and was determined to change the subject. "Why don't you need you typewriter any more, I often hear you typing when I come home from work?"

"I have written a book, and now it's all finished. Because it's finished I can go away and don't need the machine. I can go and do anything I like, there are so many things I want to try."

"You didn't tell me you'd written a book, is it very long?"

"I took it down to the printer; they said it was 350,000 words and one of the longest they had ever seen. The girl asked me if I had typed it all myself. I said I hadn't just typed it, and explained that I had "written" it and that there is a big difference. I'll go and get you the typewriter now, and that will give me a start for moving and then there will be less to do next week." I offered to go with him and said I would store the machine for a while until he wanted it back. In his flat he gave me not only the heavy black machine, but also the piles of paper onto which he had typed, or written, and we brought them all back to my room.

"Now that's made a good start, you can see that there is not really much more to clean out. All these papers you can take down to the rubbish. I had to have proper photocopies made when I took them all to the Bodleian library last week. It's a massive library and they will keep them there for hundreds of years."

"Wouldn't that be a shame if I throw away all the papers you have written, it must have taken you a very long time?"

"Yes it took me all my life really, but I managed to type it all out in just six years. You see I had to learn Greek and Sanskrit and some pages are all written by hand because I couldn't do it on a typewriter."

"Don't you want to have it published so that people can read it after so many years work?" I asked.

"Oh no, nobody will want to read it. I couldn't expect any

one to print and publish it; it's not that kind of book. Anyone who could understand it would not need to read it."

"Well, I'd certainly like to try, what is the title?" I said, leafing through a massive pile of double spaced sheets of paper.

"Oh no, it doesn't have a title, it's not that kind of a book."

"What did they say at the library when they saw it didn't have a title?"

"They didn't mind, weren't bothered at all, it's not that kind of a library. They keep a copy of everything that's written for hundreds of years, it's a sort of storehouse. They just put my name and "untitled". They made me have proper copies of everything, though, and I numbered all the pages and filled in a form. Now I've got a number, an ISBN number it's called, so it's all been done properly."

"I've heard of books without titles, but never one that's not intended to be read."

"Oh yes there have been several, you don't read them, you eat them. People don't like to eat them because they taste very bitter in the mouth and burn the stomach."

Once more I thought it time to change the subject, and asked him how he was going to get a passport.

"First of all I have to have my birth certificate and then some photos and then go to a doctor or someone for a signature. It's all quite simple these days and then I will have to go to a travel agent and buy a ticket."

Part Three: Life As A Non-Smoker

I asked him if he would like to take the travel supplement of the Sunday paper to read but he said he wasn't too bothered. "The typewriter needs a new ribbon because half of it is worn away and only the red part works because I never used that."

With that he left and shuffled his way across the little hall. As soon as he had gone I picked up the pages of his book and began to read. After the first paragraph I decided I couldn't make any sense of it at all. I tried a few pages further on but it became no clearer, there were hand drawn graphs and mystical symbols as well as whole chapters written by hand in Greek and what I presumed to be Sanskrit. There was mention of names such as Gilgamesh, Patanjali, Aristotle, Sephiroth, and Otz Chaiim, but despite trying for several hours I was completely unable to discover any theme or coherence.

It was in the evening two weeks later when he again knocked on my door.

"Hello" he said, "I've come to say goodbye. Tomorrow morning at 5.30 I am going to the airport, the flat is all clean and empty and ready for someone else."

"Did you manage to get your passport and tickets alright?"

"Oh yes, everyone has been very helpful and I have everything I need."

"I will be happy to help you with your bags to the airport in the morning."

"Oh no, I don't need any help; I haven't got any bags, just

my umbrella and my towel. I can get the number 18 bus at the bottom of the street into the main bus station and then there is a coach to Heathrow airport that leaves at seven o'clock. I have to be at the airport two hours before the flight so I am going to take some sandwiches. If you ever visit Belize you must come and say hello."

* * * * *

Yes, you do have the right book.

"But that short story had absolutely nothing to do with smoking." you say.

Quite true, why should it? You are a non-smoker and from now on you have to get used to the idea that you and smoking have nothing more to do with each other.

Good isn't it? You have recently given smoking a lot of emphasis and importance, and now it's time to let go and put it in background.

* * * * *

CONTROLLING THE WILL

This is the daily exercise No 2 and is VERY important.

Choose some simple act, such as tying three knots in a piece of string and then undoing them, or standing on one leg for a minute and then the other leg for a minute. Do this action every day at more or less the same time. The act should be something without meaning or value, merely arbitrary and the more trivial the action the more it will arouse the will. (Cleaning your shoes or taking vitamin tablets would not be suitable as they both serve a purpose.) You can repeat the same actions each day or use new ones. In the morning say to yourself "at a certain time I will do .... today"

Once you have decided on a suitable action, write this in your exercise book and put a tick for each day you manage to accomplish it. Try very hard not to miss a single day as it is the continuity of effort that is important. Remembering, finding time and mustering up the energy to do this every day is of course an exercise in itself!

TICK IN THE BOX

TOUGH MOMENTS

From time to time tough moments are going to come along, that is the nature of life which has its ups and downs. There is something wonderful about these difficult times because they provide little tests for you get past, and each time this happens you become stronger and you realise that you can actually handle every situation BETTER without a cigarette. It is almost worth quitting just for these moments, which you can treat as a game that you know you can win.

At some point you will have the most wonderful realization and say, "I got past that difficult situation without smoking, now I know I really am a non-smoker. You will never catch me with a cigarette in my mouth again, I don't want them, I don't need them and I don't like them."

*   *   *   *   *

Here is one more exercise; it is optional, enjoyable and VERY highly recommended as an aid to breaking habits.

CHANGE HAND WRITING

Take the "Begin it Now" poem by Goethe (or one of your own favourites) and write this out in a completely different handwriting. Make your letters much larger or smaller than usual, try using a broader nib, slope letters forwards or make them more upright, perhaps you can try some decorative design on the capital letters.

You can do this in your notebook or you might want to spend more time and do it really beautifully on a special sheet of paper. The chances are that you formed your handwriting at a stage in your life that you have out grown and now is a good time to make a change.

Spending time on this exercise will affect your life for years to come – it really is well worth finding the time to sit down and do it properly. Go to town; buy some calligraphy pens and ink or Japanese brushes together with good quality paper and a little book that gives examples. You can also experiment with Celtic patterns and Mandalas which will provide hours of relaxing fun.

Decide how often and when you are going to do this exercise, perhaps establish a weekly rhythm which brings discipline and stability into your life, the more frequently you can do it the better.

TICK IN THE BOX

Habit is stronger than reason and just thinking about change is not sufficient, you have to DO something, you have to use your body and your will.

CHANGES IN MY HEALTH

Now is the time to start looking for those promised health improvements, some of which can start appearing very quickly.

Almost certainly you have noticed an increase in energy, and it is good to transform this with physical exercise, otherwise it might bottle up and try to come out in the form of anger or bad temper. It may well be that you are waking earlier and need less sleep.

- Sperm count up. (I am not sure how you do the mathematics on this one but the experts say it happens!)
- Look at the colour of your tongue.
- Look at the colour of your gums.
- Look at the white of your eyes
- Look at the pink colour under your fingernails

Then more gradually you can look for;

- Difference in the quality of your hair
- Difference in the quality of your skin
- Less dark under you eyes
- Teeth staying whiter

Apart from all this there are certainly great changes happening to your blood and every one of your internal organs. Your tongue and gums can give an acupuncturist, dentist or doctor an indication of what is going on inside, and you can tell a lot about your own general health by making careful observations of your mouth and tongue.

With all these changes going on it makes sense to eat properly and drink pure water as well as to take some good quality vitamin tablets, you are building up a whole new body completely free from nicotine poisoning so give yourself the best chance possible. You should be feeling fitter and be in better shape and that makes life more enjoyable.

Other people might well notice changes that you have not detected yourself, for example increased confidence, that you have become less opinionated or generally more pleasant to be with.

Write these things and other observation in your notebook, indeed it might well have become a diary by now as this could well be a very interesting turning point in your life. If you have been taking the exercises seriously there could be many more subtle changes happening, perhaps to your dream life, your sex life, or the breaking of some other habits and the development of completely new interests.

One of the most amazing phenomena is that it is possible for your voice to change after six months or so. As you are instantly recognizable through your voice for this to alter indicates a truly remarkable change in personality.

Keep up with your physical exercise regime as you need the

fresh air and extra oxygen. It will be good if you can treat yourself to a sauna or steam bath from time to time and feel the nicotine poison leaving your body, perhaps you can enjoy a relaxing massage afterwards. You might well have conversations with other people there who have also stopped and be fascinated to learn how much their lives have changed.

You will certainly have some extra money which has to be good news, and your breath, clothes, hair, house and car no longer smell of stale tobacco. Friends and family have said some very kind and encouraging things too, life is good as a non-smoker, you certainly made the right decision.

This might be an interesting time to go out and observe smokers in bars and cafes. Don't be frightened to do this as for most people there is no danger at all that you will feel inclined to have a smoke with them. You can see now that they really don't enjoy smoking at all, one dissatisfying cigarette after another, a craving which feeds upon itself, the drug that gives nothing, it is all very sad. Without a doubt they are a lovely bunch of people but there is absolutely nothing in this particular activity of theirs for you to envy.

Have a look at some of the other good things that are happening now you have stopped and write them all down in your notebook, you should be feeling stronger, healthier and happier with a more positive attitude to life.

TIPS REGARDING THE EXERCISES

Before doing the exercises turn off the radio and TV, slow down your breathing, and use them as an opportunity to bring a few minutes of peace and quiet to your life. Do not think of them as being specifically aids to stopping smoking, treat them in the same way as you do the other steps you are taking to improve your general health and well being.

END A RELATIONSHIP

You can perhaps consider quitting tobacco in the same way as you end an uncomfortable or unrewarding relationship. You have been living with nicotine for a long time, now this has suddenly gone leaving a space and it will take a while before all traces of it have completely disappeared. Nature dislikes a vacuum and something else will come into your life so try to develop a few good habits.

Make sure that when the desire for nicotine pops up you can say "Um, that's all ended, I do not want to think about that now, perhaps I will later on tonight although it isn't very important", or "The time I spent smoking was the wrong thing for me, it never did me any good, I have now moved forward, I have far, far better things to do with my time and money."

* * * * *

Buy some more flowers, be thankful.

* * * * *

Here is the third and last daily exercise followed by other examples of things that you can do to break habits.

EXERCISE NO. 3

In the morning and evening when you clean your teeth, do so using your left hand (sorry left-handed people). This sounds very simple, and indeed it is, but you might not always remember! This takes no extra time at all, and when you don't forget it is very effective, so please do it.

Write in your notebook that you intend to do this for a set length of time, and record how long you have gone without missing a day.

TICK IN THE BOX.

*　　*　　*　　*　　*

HABIT BREAKING

To make anything a habit, do it.
To not make it a habit, do not do it.
To unmake a habit, do something else in place of it

Epictetus, 60-110AD

It was promised that the exercises would not take more than five minutes a day but you might well consider it prudent to spend extra time on them. Here are some more suggestions for the type of things that you can do to end habits in general.

Make efforts to replace your bad habits with good ones, do simple things like putting your shoes away neatly and by generally paying attention to "small things". This should be fun and enjoyable or at very least pleasant.

Next time you go shopping give your self a change by buying a completely different type of toothpaste, soap and shampoo. After cleaning your teeth in the evening, hide the toothpaste from yourself and put the soap in an unusual place. Try to have a little laugh if you are unable to find them (it is best not to try this one with your car keys).

- Change your name. (This is a very big and very dramatic move).
- Use a different cup at breakfast and sit in another place.
- Walk backwards for thirty yards a day, be careful.
- Go a different route to work
- Make your bed before breakfast/breakfast before bed
- Redecorate your room
- Turn your notebook into a diary. This is very good.
- There must still be a few old things you can chuck out!
- Meet new people and find new interests

- Fill your feeling life, paint, draw, sing, dance, join a theatre club.
- Help other people, look after some animals or plants
- Lose yourself to find yourself.
- Change your hair style
- Go up stairs two at a time, or one step and then two steps.
- Move your bed into a new position
- Buy a different newspaper sometimes.
- Knit as a new hobby, it keeps the hands busy and you end up with beautiful pullovers.

The stopping process will be much easier when you use these little exercises and you may well notice some other habits falling by the wayside. Spending time on the exercises will be of enormous benefit and it is good if you can invent some of your own.

It is best not to overload yourself, but make sure that you do the three most important ones properly every day, of course finding time and remembering to do them is also an exercise.

REVIEW OF EXERCISES

No1 write a sentence with your left hand

No2 will exercise

No3 clean your teeth with other hand.

The next most important is to change your hand writing, if you really can not spare a few minutes for this every day do it at weekends and thus establish a weekly rhythm.

Keep finding and jettisoning clutter.

* * * * *

By smoking you have been performing the same action many times each day perhaps for years, and there can be no doubt that this has became a deeply ingrained habit. Nicotine addiction is a very small part of the problem, it is the habit and psychological brainwashing that need to be removed or replaced, and time spent now is going to make a real difference for the rest of your life – five minutes is the minimum time you should be spending on the exercises.

* * * * *

Who is strong? He who controls his passions.

Judaism Mishnah, Abot 4.1

PART FOUR

YOU HAVE STOPPED FOR GOOD

Well you have accomplished something wonderful, you have stopped smoking, and you have done it by yourself.

How do you feel? What is the emotion sweeping over you? It could well be one of utter relief, relief that you are free and don't have to be bothered by smoking any more. Life is certainly more enjoyable when you are not attached to a ball and chain. You don't have to tick off the number of days that you have stopped because now you are out of prison; it's the people still trapping themselves inside who need to count the days until their release.

Having got this far and taken a step into the future, it really is essential to make sure there is no relapse; involve your family and friends as much as possible, they will be delighted you have stopped and will want to provide support and encouragement. If you would rather they don't say anything or make a fuss, let them know and they will be pleased to cooperate.

Keep on with the exercises for several weeks as they do a lot to make the process easier. If you have found them helpful treat yourself to copies of *Knowledge of Higher Worlds* and *Occult Science*, where further exercises are given together with an explanation of how, when and why they can be incorporated into your daily life.

You might well have met people who after having success-fully stopped smoking for years and years suddenly started again! This seems like absolute madness and is incredibly hard to believe when you have so recently quit but sadly it happens. People think they have developed an immunity and can smoke – "just one" cigarette. Oh NO, "one cigarette" is all it takes to get back into the habit, learn from their mistake do not ever, ever, EVER have another cigarette. You have not stopped for just a few days, a few weeks a few months or a few years, you have stopped FOR GOOD, you are a non-smoker. Non-smokers do not smoke. Tobacco and you have nothing more to do with each other.

*   *   *   *   *

When being offered a cigarette it is a wonderful thing to say for the first time, "No thank you, I don't smoke", just make sure that you keep on saying it

PANGS

It really is not surprising that after doing the same thing, twenty times a day, for X number of years and suddenly stopping that the old habit reappears from time to time. This shows just how badly you were hooked and how necessary it was to remove nicotine from your life. This little pang is just an intrusion to which you say "I am certainly not going to mourn your parting, please go away, you are not part of my life, I am much, much better off without you". The pangs become smaller and less frequent and the stopping gets easier. Instead of "I want a cigarette", you need to take a couple of breaths of fresh air and say "I certainly do NOT want a cigarette, I do not smoke".

A good length of time will pass before you go a whole day without missing a cigarette, this is quite normal and to be expected. Don't worry if at some point during the day you start thinking about nicotine, just say to yourself, "Oh no, I don't want to think about that now, perhaps later on tonight. It's really not important, right now I want to concentrate on cooking supper."

*　*　*　*　*

Strange isn't it going out and not having to worry about taking cigarettes and a lighter? This is how life is meant to be, you were born a non-smoker.

IN CASE OF EMERGENCY

Have you taken advantage of all the suggestions and exercises given here? They have worked perfectly well up until now and they will work again. Read through all your "reasons for stopping", and for "not starting again" – they are still valid – then go for a walk even if it is raining, snowing or very hot, and read them again when you come back if necessary. Probably the pang will have gone away.

Is this a real emergency? Perhaps you are simply trying to use this moment of stress as an excuse to start again. Don't.

The trick is not to give your old smoking habit any importance; it's a thing of the past and no longer part of your life. You have far, far better things to do than think about cigarettes and you have now stopped for a sufficient length of time to know full well that you don't need to start again.

Stopping the pleasant way doesn't mean that you will start living a problem-free life; you will still have good days and bad. You can manage perfectly well without nicotine poison in your body and you know that it is no longer part of the NEW YOU, it is out of character, it's gone, finished. Smoking doesn't suit you.

Do you really think that one little puff of smoke can possibly solve your problems or relieve your stress? It is nonsense. It's what those wretched tobacco companies have been telling you for years and years, but it is not true. One cigarette makes you want another and the old record starts playing again, the problem's not physical, it's mental. You have not got one good reason to start again.

Part Four: You Have Stopped For Good

As explained above, after a long time smoking several cigarettes each day for an extended period there are certainly going to be some little pangs for a cigarette from time to time. You might think that you need just half a cigarette or even one tiny little puff. Habit, ritual, addiction is all involved and can all be dealt with, the silly pang will not last long.

Take a few deep breaths and bring some clean fresh air into your already healing lungs; do not start making them dirty again. Go for another little walk, listen to the birds, take a shower or bath or sauna, the moment will surely pass this time as it has before.

For some people it helps to go to a smoking environment and see people "enjoying" one cigarette after another as an example of "what not to do". It's amazing to think even for one moment that you would volunteer to smoke twenty or more cigarettes a day. These people are fine and lovely, let them smoke away, but avoid it yourself. Save your health and save some money.

Do you really think you want a filthy cigarette? You won't like it, it will burn your tongue, taste horrible, make you cough, make you feel sick and dizzy and you will be doing long term damage to yourself. Next day your mouth will be dry, your clothes and hair will smell awful and you will feel terrible. Get over this difficult moment and you will be much stronger to face the future. That's the wonderful bit, get over this hurdle and you will know that you can get over the next and the next, and even look forward to the challenge. Stopping does become easier and easier, life really does become better.

Take a good look at your health checks too; it doesn't take long for your health to improve. Don't go backwards – your lungs are doing much, much better without being coated in smoke and tar. One cigarette is the thin end of the wedge, the first step on the slippery downhill path. It's your life, your health, your decision, and it affects you much more than anyone else.

One cigarette will certainly lead to another and it's too simple to start smoking again.

Take a good look at your notebook and read the excellent reasons for stopping and for not starting again. Has anything changed? No.

Stay a non-smoker, you made the right decision, you have stopped for good.

FRIENDS OF NICOTINE

Associated with nicotine were a group of friends such as coffee, alcohol, tea, and cannabis who liked to gather around the same table. You might want to stop some or all of these completely for a while, say three weeks, as they can act as a reminder of old times. It will also be good to know that you can live happily without their company, and after a set time you can decide if you want to reintroduce them. The main thing now is to ensure that you do not start smoking again.

There is an advantage to having a Detox Programme or total blitz, cutting out alcohol, coffee, tea and cigarettes all in one go. This is very much your decision but with the exercises given you may be surprised just how easy it can be.

CANNABIS

This book is for people who "want to stop smoking" which is generally taken to mean cigarettes, cigars, and pipes with tobacco. Times have changed considerably and now in many countries cannabis is smoked openly and is as freely available as alcohol. There are people who think they have stopped smoking tobacco but smoke 25 joints a day. Perhaps it is nicotine that they are after.

Social functions often have wine, beer, cannabis, and tobacco as norms. At one time we were told by well intentioned people that soft drugs could lead to harder ones. Times change, it now seems that cannabis can lead to nicotine addiction and young people can indeed become dependent on nicotine because they have been introduced to it mixed with cannabis.

It is very hard to smoke tobacco in moderation, "stop smoking" means "stop smoking." Many people want to continue to smoke cannabis but don't want to smoke tobacco and this presents a very real dilemma as they are combined to make a joint. Once there is a genuine desire to stop smoking cannabis, the exercises in this book will be beneficial. There is no smoke without fire.

GREEN ISSUES

Tobacco is a strange crop that the world could well do without; it requires fertile land which would be better employed growing food for people who really need it, hungry people. Not only are vast acres of good farmland necessary to produce tobacco but even more acres of woodland, particularly in Africa, are felled and used in the drying process.

Pollution is caused by the transportation of tons and tons of cigarettes – in France alone an incredible 8000 tons of tobacco is smoked each year.

People looking for ethical investments generally make sure they exclude tobacco companies and the banks that cooperate with them.

STOPPED BUT NOT CONTENT

It is possible for people who have stopped, using other methods, to feel uncomfortable and that they are "missing something" and even people who have quit for several months can live fighting a continual uphill battle. If you are in this position do not start again but read slowly through this book right from the beginning. Follow the plan step by step, make entries in your notebook as much as you can and partake in all the exercises taking particular care to list all the positive aspects of having stopped. You will find that your decision to stop is enforced and that the quality of your life improves. It might be that you are still using gums, patches, herbal cigarettes etc, think about quitting these as they tend to act as a constant reminder that you are not smoking. You have done well to stop, you have got this book in your hands, give it a try, you have everything to gain and nothing to lose. Stopping is pleasant.

TRIED TO STOP SO MANY TIMES THAT I AM RESIGNED TO BEING A SMOKER FOR THE REST OF MY LIFE

You have tried many times before which means that you WANT to stop. You can certainly start reading this and other books which might well motivate you into trying once more, most people have several attempts before stopping. Take it slowly, don't expect too much too quickly, make little experiments with the exercises and begin to look after other aspects of your health by eating fresh foods, and increasing your physical exercise. The little exercises given in this book are an effective aid to daily living, but only when you do them.

What may seem a small step for others can be a big step for you. Giving up anything, even half a spoonful of sugar in your coffee, on a regular daily basis will go a long way to increasing self confidence and once you have done it for months, or even years, you will know that you can control your habits. Try writing out a favourite piece of poetry in a completely different handwriting, do this weekly, as it is the perseverance and constant endeavour that makes you strong.

Keep an open mind about the possibility of stopping, don't give in, your opportunity will come one day – perhaps when you least expect it. Try saying and writing out something like this:

"I will forget that I failed last time and try once more as if it never happened. There is so much strength in me and the world that can lift and carry me towards a more healthy life."

You are not condemned to a life of smoking; there is a technique and a time for you. Only when you try will you succeed.

* * * * *

I DON'T WANT TO STOP

This book has been written for people who do want to stop.

* * * * *

HELPING PEOPLE STOP AND NOT STARTING

It is wonderful to have the question "How do I help other people?" but not always easy to know how to go about it. While more and more people are successfully managing to stop smoking young people are still starting. The desire to help loved ones or friends who smoke is quite understandable but presents numerous difficulties, they are adults living out their own lives, discovering their destiny, doing some things right and making some mistakes. It is particularly disconcerting when your own offspring are attracted to nicotine and other nasties, indeed having the courage to let them "be free" can be the most challenging phase of parenthood.

You are rightly concerned but there is a real danger that if you do nag and bully they will stop nicotine and replace it with something even more harmful. Saying "Don't smoke" can sometimes act as a challenge. The forbidden can become attractive.

Once people have stopped warm encouragement is generally welcomed and most people appreciate a little praise.

Just what can be done to help teenagers experimenting with cigarettes? During their time at school they have been well informed of the dangers of smoking but each generation is more adventurous with drugs in general and youngsters have money to spend. This book has a definite starting point, it's for people who want to stop and the task has clearly been to help people strengthen their resolve. This is by far the easier side of the stop smoking question and if there is not yet a resolve to stop then the problem is very different. One solution is to try to substitute a worthwhile interest, for example sport, study, learning an instrument or joining a choir. Interest is the key word.

TEENAGERS

If you are a teenager reading this and contemplating trying smoking you should be able to realise that there are lots of adults who wish they had never started and are desperately trying to stop. At your age they thought they would not become hooked and they were in for a nasty surprise, now they are buying books like this to help them break what has become a very serious habit. No smoker will ever recommend tobacco, it is not cool, it is not glamorous and it doesn't make you attractive. There are much better things to do with your money and by far the best solution is never to start in the first place. Smoking is an experience you can do without and you can be a lot smarter than the previous generations, when you are a parent in a few years time you will be saying exactly the same thing.

Nicotine may be legal but it is one of many dangerous drugs and you are far better off not smoking.

*   *   *   *   *

PART FIVE

RUDOLF STEINER & THE BASIC EXCERCISES

Any one familiar with the works of Dr. Rudolf Steiner will almost certainly realize that the "Will-Exercise" given here has been adapted from his book *Occult Science, an Outline*. Some of the other exercises, such as changing handwriting, were also taken from his books and lectures.

Writing an introduction to Rudolf Steiner (the founder of Anthroposophy or Spiritual Science), and his works to those completely unfamiliar with him would be a daunting task and not one that is going to be undertaken here. The "Will-Exercise", however, is so central to the effectiveness of this book that some mention should be made of its source.

The reason for this is three-fold.

1.   This exercise was given as one of a "total package" of five exercises, listed briefly below, which were intended to be used alongside each other.

2.   Rudolf Steiner pointed out that the exercises go parallel with making progress in the ethical or moral sphere.

3.   While one can simply undertake the exercises on an "I do them because they work basis" a scientific explanation was given and we are encouraged to discover both "how" and "why" they work.

Occult Science is a lengthy book which speaks about world origins and the great events of evolution, towards its close exercises are given which have become known as the "Accessory exercises" or "Nebenubungen". *Occult Science* is deliberately not written in an easy style and Rudolf Steiner intended the very reading of it as an initial step in spiritual training, inasmuch as the necessary effort of quiet thought and contemplation strengthens the powers of the soul and develops a closeness with the spiritual world.

The exercises were given to cultivate control over thoughts, (in their course and sequence) over will, and over feelings, as a path to knowledge of the higher worlds. Further exercises for self development were given in various books and lectures particularly in "Knowledge of the Higher Worlds and how it is attained"

* * * * *

A very short introduction to THE FIVE "ACCESSORY EXERCISES" as given in *Occult Science*

WILL EXERCISE

In *Occult Science* we read, "a good exercise for the will is, every day for months on end, to give oneself the command: "Today you are to do "this", at this particular hour". One will gradually manage to fix the hour and the nature of the task so as to render the command perfectly possible to carry out."

CONCENTRATION

Direct your thought, for at least five minutes daily, and for months on end to some commonplace object, for example a needle or a pencil – and shut out during those five minutes all thoughts that have no connection with the object. (This is far from easy!)

FEELING/EQUANIMITY

Learn to control the outward expression of joy and sorrow. In doing this you will discover that you do not grow less but actually more sensitive than before to everything in your environment that can arouse emotions of joy and pain. Here we try to avoid swinging between sympathy and antipathy toward what comes to us from outside. Instead, we try to maintain a balance between the two extremes. By consciously paying attention to our reactions we come to see how letting ourselves be swayed from side to side prevents us from seeing the true nature of whatever meets us and we become more receptive to what lives in our environment.

We endeavour to retain composure in the face of joy and sorrow, and eradicate the tendency to fluctuate between the seventh heaven of joy and the depths of despair.

POSITIVENESS

A lovely legend is related of Christ Jesus. It tells how He is walking with a few other persons, and they pass a dead dog. The others turn away from the revolting sight. Christ Jesus speaks admiringly of the beautiful teeth of the animal. One can train oneself to meet the world with the disposition of soul that this legend displays.

To cultivate this soul attitude does not mean to avoid all criticism; close our eyes to what is bad, false, inferior. It is not possible to find the bad *good*, and the false *true*. It *does mean* to attain an attitude of sympathetically entering into any situation so as to see its best attributes.

OPENMINDEDNESS AND PARTIALITY

Readiness to meet life with an open mind recognizing that every opinion has a certain validity, though it may be extremely difficult to see. Above all, we should not reject opinions because they run counter to the ideas and practices generally accepted in our environment.

"I never heard of such a thing, I don't believe it!" should make no sense at all to a pupil of the Spirit. Rather let him make the deliberate resolve, during a certain period of time to let everything or being he encounters tell him something new. A breath of wind, a leaf falling from a tree, the prattle of a little child, can all teach us something.

COMBINATION OF ALL FIVE TO FORM A SIXTH

Practise the above in manifold combinations – #1 plus #2, #3 plus #4, etc. in order to establish harmony among them. It will also of course be helpful to study the books from which they are taken

*　*　*　*　*

"These exercises are suitable for anyone to do who is in earnest about it," said Rudolf Steiner. "The important point is not to aim for any special achievement such as attaining 'spiritual vision,' 'enlightenment,' or the like, but to keep steadily going in the direction one has chosen, regardless of results Whereas the usual attitude in our material world is to 'go get,' to accomplish, spiritual results come of themselves when we practice steadily. Spiritual qualities, their value, come to us, but only when we are ready to receive them; to bear them. The movement is reversed."

He said also, 'When these exercises are conscientiously carried out it will be found that they yield, gradually, much more than at first appeared to be in them."

*　*　*　*　*

It is continuity of effort that builds the power of control

*　*　*　*　*

FOR PEOPLE WHO HAVE
STOPPED SMOKING

Now we are all in the same position, thank goodness, because we have all stopped smoking and know it is a wonderful and liberating accomplishment. It doesn't really matter when we stopped the important thing is that we are sure we will not start again. Well done, you must be delighted. I hope that one day you will find yourself in the position of saying, "Oh, I stopped smoking years ago, no problem at all after the first few weeks, best thing I ever did." or you might completely forget that you were ever a smoker! That will be marvellous.

This book was written specifically for people who want to stop smoking and this little chapter is written for those who have actually done so. I truly hope that there are thousands upon thousands of people reading this and I would love to see the day when cigarette manufacturing is a thing of the past as it has already killed and maimed far too many people. Smoking really is a silly and expensive way to kill yourself and we have proved that stopping is possible and that it improves the quality of life.

Smokers struggle desperately to find some justification for their habit and know that what they are doing is not wise; understandably they resent being told that which they already know. It is often very difficult to give a smoker a "Stop Smoking" book and if they do manage to start reading one it can often rub them up the wrong way and make them upset and angry. When I was still a smoker I can remember several occasions when my well intentioned Mother, Aunt

Agnes and Uncle Fred all tried to give me such books and I was very hasty in rejecting their advice. It was a subject I was not ready to face or discuss. I had tried a few times to stop, or at least cut down, as I knew somewhere deep inside me that I had a real problem with a very nasty drug. I took a long time to wake up and face up.

Everybody has to discover their own way of stopping with or without a book. The method that I used has been described; clear motivation, facing the problem honestly, looking for the positive aspects of stopping and employing very powerful exercises to make and reinforce the decision. This is a sensible workable approach and has been used successfully by many people. I have listened carefully to a multitude of smokers around the world and gathered a great deal of information about nicotine addiction. As a middle aged male it has been particularly important to try to gain a female perspective and to become aware of the experiences of people both younger and older than myself so that the book could be adapted accordingly. Much credit must go to Dr Rudolf Steiner for the wonderful exercises which appear so simple and help so much.

This book avoids nagging because it only addresses people who know they want to stop and when you know what you want you stand a fair chance of getting it. Nagging is not helpful, it doesn't work and it can lead people to replace nicotine with drugs that are even more dangerous. The chances of stopping when you are still able to find something positive about nicotine are small and at some point you come to the realisation that you must stop "one day" so it might as well be "right now". Anyway that is all history for you, you did it and you did it your way.

I was aware that some readers think they will never be able to stop and that they can become very despondent. I wanted to give them every encouragement to keep on trying and at the same time tell other readers it is easy and pleasant. A very difficult task! We are indeed complex creatures capable of fooling ourselves by setting our alarm clocks five minutes early or our watches five minutes late. With smoking we tell ourselves it is easy to stop, do it, and then discover that it is true! Most people have had several attempts before stopping completely and I believe that by continuing methodically with the exercises the day comes when everyone can find the strength and courage to stop. *"Providence moves too."*

It is dreadfully sad that so many young people continue to start smoking despite having been told repeatedly at home and at school that it is unhealthy. With much better education, more awareness and considerably less advertising than in earlier generations this is unfortunate. Being a teenager in this modern world is increasingly difficult, they are vulnerable targets for all sorts of commercial and peer pressures and are making exactly the same mistake that we did a few years earlier. Nicotine traps you so cleverly, we know that the answer is never to start and we must search for a way to impart this to younger people. Your best friend doesn't tell you only what you want to hear and to have at least one person say "cigarettes are not necessary, you are better off without them" is perhaps no bad thing. Smokers do tend to listen to doctors, nurses, dentists and people like you, who have stopped.

Thank you very much for reading this book, I am so glad that you too are a non-smoker!

Works by Dr Rudolf Steiner recommended for further reading:

Occult Science, an outline
Knowledge of Higher Worlds and how it is achieved
Overcoming Nervousness
From Comets to Cocaine ISBN185584088X

Available from Rudolf Steiner Press and The Anthroposophic Press